Mother's Milk

By Common Consent Press is a non-profit publisher dedicated to producing affordable, high-quality books that help define and shape the Latter-day Saint experience. BCC Press publishes books that address all aspects of Mormon life. Our mission includes finding manuscripts that will contribute to the lives of thoughtful Latter-day Saints, mentoring authors and nurturing projects to completion, and distributing important books to the Mormon audience at the lowest possible cost.

Mother's Milk
Poems in Search of Heavenly Mother

Written by
Rachel Hunt Steenblik

Illustrated by
Ashley Mae Hoiland

BCC
PRESS

For information contact
By Common Consent Press
4062 S. Evelyn Dr.
Salt Lake City, UT 84124-2250

Cover design: Ralph Steenblik with D. Christian Harrison
Cover illustration: Ashley Mae Hoiland
Book design: Andrew Heiss

www.bccpress.org

ISBN-10: 0-9986052-2-0
ISBN-13: 978-0-9986052-2-7

10 9 8 7 6 5 4 3 2 1

Rachel
For my children, Cora and Søren,
my parents, Claudia and Larry, and all those
who hunger for Heavenly Mother.

AshMae
To the women who first asked me to speak
the words Heavenly Mother, specifically
Rachel, who wrote these poems. Sara for
encouraging me to continue to say those
words and to learn of Her, and my children,
Remy, Thea and Luna, for whom I will always
say those beloved words aloud as we know
Her more and more.

Contents

—

Acknowledgements

Rachel   I have the lucky problem of having too many people to thank. Among them are David Paulsen, Martin Pulido, Caroline Kline, Elizabeth Pinborough, Naomi Win, Maxwell Institute, Claudia and Richard Bushman, Claudia and Larry Hunt, Melody Newey Johnson, Brooke Jones Williams, Jessica Ecker, Jan Marie Anderson, Charity Hunt, Kathy West, Missy McConkie, Carol Ann Litster Young, Michelle Larson, Brittany and Dane Thorley, Ashley Mae Hoiland, Jacob Baker, Blaire Ostler, Poesis, Exponent II, Naomi Watkins, Annie K. Blake, Emily Brown, Jason Kerr, Spencer Steenblik, Kristine Haglund, Michael Austin, Steve Evans, Tracy McKay, Kyle Monson, BCC Press, Andrew Heiss, Blair Hodges, Christian Harrison, Meg Porter, and always Cora and Søren Steenblik. While individual contributions varied, each gave me inspiration, encouragement, and instruction. I thank them. I could not have written *Mother's Milk* without them.

AshMae   Thank you, Rachel, for allowing me to be a part of this project. We'd talked about it so many years ago; it is an honor to work with you. The wonderful, patient and encouraging people at the BCC Press. In particular, Michael Austin, Steve Evans, Kristine Haglund, and Tracy Mckay who have dedicated time and love to this project. Andrew Heiss for typesetting the manuscript. Thank you to the many people behind the scenes who have supported the project and the first publications at BCC Press.

Introduction

These are the poems that I could write with my questions, my hurt, my hope, and my reaching. Others could write other poems with theirs. I hope that they will. We need them all.

When the child is to be weaned, the mother, too, is not without sorrow, because she and the child are more and more to be separated, because the child who first lay under her heart and later rested upon her breast will never again be so close. So they grieve together the brief sorrow. How fortunate the one who kept the child so close and did not need to grieve any more!

—Søren Aabye Kierkegaard

Invocation
Dear God,
May I know
the Mother as
She knows me,
may I love Her as
She loves me.
In Jesus' name,
amen.

The Hunger

Motherless Milk

I searched for my Mother, the way a baby roots
for her mother's breast, head nuzzling from side to side,
mouth open, ready to suckle. But I was still thirsty.
Then my belly grew, and my breasts grew, and
a ravenous little thing came out. I offer her my milk
without money and without price. My husband
offered it to her once, while I sat beside them on a train.
She pursed her lips against the false nipple,
and stared at me with sad eyes. I wondered then,
if Heavenly Mother walked into another room
so we would take the bottle. I wondered then,
if we are weaned.

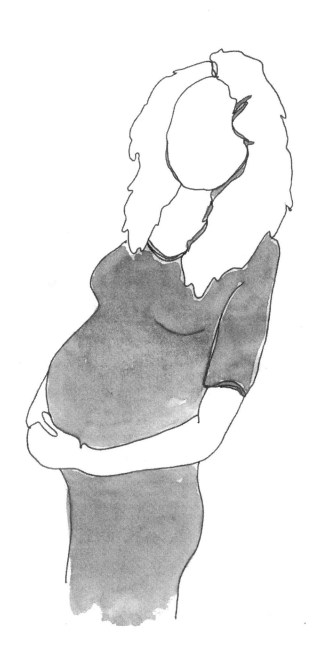

What Søren Aabye Taught Me
When the child needed to be weaned,
the Mother cried.

How She Broke Her Own Heart
The Mother held me tightly
and said, *I'm sorry,*
Mama's milk is all gone,
as I sobbed and sobbed.

The Very Hungry Girl
One Monday evening, the
cool moon came up, and out
of the womb came a tiny and
very hungry girl. She started to
look for her Mother.

Questions

I asked my daughter two questions
the day that she was born.
1) Did she remember me—
   my voice, my smell,
   my beating heart?
2) Did she remember the one
   we both call Mother—
   Her voice, Her Smell, Her heart?
I can't remember anything.

Separation Anxiety
On Her daughter's
first day of Earth,
they both wept.

The Third Comforter
When night fell, the
Papa tried to console
His daughter, but it
didn't work; she
wanted Mama.

The Child
She can sleep
without her Mother,
but she doesn't want to.

Story Time
The Mother
can read me
anything.
(I just want
to hear Her
voice.)

Bedtime Routine
The Mother isn't here, to
read me stories, and
tuck me in, and tell me
She loves me. So I
read my own stories, and
tuck myself in, and
whisper, *I love you,*
into the dark.

What Søren Taught Me
Sons also
search for their
Mothers.

Lost Boys
What Peter Pan's
Lost Boys
lost was
their Mother.

Lost Girl
What Peter did not
know, is that
the Lost Girl, like
the Lost boys,
needed a Mother.

What Every Child Wants to Know
What every child wants to know is
if her Mother is watching.
What every child wants to know is
if she is seen.

Peek-a-Boo
Sometimes we play
Peek-a-Boo.
I laugh at first, delighted.
Where's Mama? She cries,
hands covering Her.
Here I am! She cries,
hands uncovering Her.
But soon I grow weary.

Again, My Toddler Gives Voice

I want my Mommy!
I want my Mommy!
I want my Mommy!

Frantic

The Mother heard Her daughter
frantic, whimper-crying,
I don't know where
to find my Mommy!

(She stepped out as
Her husband stepped in, but
Their daughter could not
see Him.)

Absent Mothers
Libby thinks absent
mothers show up in
children's stories
because it is the
scariest thing a child
can think, and it can be
thought by any child.
I think that she is right.

Fairy God Mother
I don't need a fairy
godmother to come,
with glass slippers, a
carriage, and dress, only a
God Mother, with wisdom,
grace, and love.

Sometimes
Sometimes
I just
need my
Mama.

(Sometimes
it is hard for Her
to be so
needed.)

Lost Lady
Margaret holds
long memories of the
lost temple, the
Lady, Asherah, the
seven-branch
lamp, the
Tree of Life.

Amiri

When the Mother will not come
to be counted, I count
the void She leaves.

Holes
Desiree was born
with a hole in her heart,
the size of an eye.
My heart has a hole,
the size of my Mother.

Home
She is what I mean,
when I say, *I want
to go home.*

What Carol Taught Me
The whys women
need the Goddess are
many—to affirm their
bodies and cycles, their
menstruation and
birthgiving, their
care for the young
and dying.

What Rosemary Taught Me

It counts how we
God-talk.
He, Him, His.
She, Her, Hers.
They, Them, Theirs.

It counts how we
God-image.
Almighty father.
Nursing mother.
Partnered parents.

Unmothered

Each of us can answer
what it is like
to lose a Mother,
to lose the one
who gave us life.

First Grief
When I lost Her,
I scribbled the words,
I think this is what grief
feels like.

Every Day
I woke up again
without my Mother.

Marco Polo
The Mother and I play
Marco Polo.
First I cry, *Marco,*
and my Mother, *Polo.*
(I am searching for Her.)
Then She cries, *Marco,*
and I, *Polo.*
(She is reaching for me.)

The Reaching

Marco Polo, II

After the firmament
was created, I
yelled, *Marco.*
The Mother
answered, *Polo,*
and I swam
faster and faster.

Messengers

I am looking for
messengers from my
Mother, to teach me.

Looking For My Mother
I am looking for my Mother,
to give me Her wisdom
richer than silver and gold.

The Woman in the Wilderness
Is She the woman
in the wilderness
who is nourished
there, or the God
who prepared
her place?

The Woman in the Moon
My brother dreamt
he carved the moon
into the shape of a woman.

Out of the Mouth of Babes
Meg talks with tiny children about our Mother.
They are so curious about it, she reports,
and they ask all of the questions that I have,
so unabashedly.

Are You My Mother?
A tiny bird and I
are in search of
our Mother.

Crawl
The child can crawl now.
One day she'll walk,
run, jump, dance.
Will she still look back
to find her Mother?
Will she still crawl onto
Her godly lap?

Where is the Mama?
When Abbi was two, she
asked *Where's da mama*
in this story? (about every story)
When I was twenty-four,
I borrowed her question.

Supplication
A baby,
calling out
in the night
for her Mother.
The first
primordial call.

Non-fiction
Lisa wrote "Irreversible
Things," reversed, including:
*The first thing I always do
when I wake up is look for
my Mother.*

Looking For You
If I knew where to find you,
I would climb out of bed,
cry, *Mama*, until I saw you.

Mommy

Cora says

Mommy,

Mommy,

Mommy,

like a prayer.

Are You There, God?

It's me, Rachel.

Mother Tongue

Cora sticks her fingers
in my mouth, <u>to learn
my language</u>. When
I let her, she laughs.
Did I do this
with my Mother?

The Glistening Expanse of Sea
On hard days,
we walk to the ocean
to find the Mother—
to watch the waves,
to smell the salt,
to feel the wind,
to hear Her speak.

If I Could Write a Letter
Dear Mama,
I miss you.
Do you miss me?
xo,
Rachel

Breathe

I tiptoe quietly into my
daughter's room, to see if
she's still breathing. Her
chest rises and falls, a
hand moves. She sighs.

I tiptoe quietly into my
Mother's heaven, to see if
She's still breathing.
Her chest rises and falls, a
hand moves. I sigh.

Follow Your Nose
Cora knows
where to find me
by my smell.
(She can do it
in her sleep.)

Do I know where
to find my Mother
by Hers?
(I do it in
my dreams.)

She smells like every
good thing—
hyacinth and honey,
lavender and lemons,
mint and basil.

rning to
 the good

The Learning

Tired
The Mother
loves us,
but She is
tired.

Her Lineage
The Mother was born
of Her Mother,
who was born
of Her Mother,
who was born…

The Hour She Learned She was God

When Her hour
came, She prayed
to be delivered,
before remembering
the Deliverer
was She.

Tree Rings

If we cut Her open,
we could count Her rings
and know Her age,
but we'd also learn Her hunger—
the years She put Her roots down deep
and threw Her arms to the sky,
and how She carried them
with grace.

Her Age
She is older
than the earth.

The Great She Is
The Mother is present.
(And past. And future.)

In the Beginning
The Mother
sang a lullaby
and there was
Light.

First Song
The Mother doesn't remember if
She cried when Her first spirit child was
born, though She does remember
crying when She sang Him the First Song.

She Laid the Measures Thereof
She was there
when the foundations
of the earth were laid,
when the morning stars
sang together and all
the daughters of God
shouted for joy.

The Mother is an Old Astronomer
She counts the stars
and names them.
She knows each one;
She sees their light.

Her Body
Her body is celestial—
as bright as the sun,
as warm as the moon.

Her body waxes
and wanes—
a sign of health,
of life.

Luna
She is the
gentlest light,
and kind,
offering brave
hope in
the darkness.

Ancient of Nights
Among the great and mighty ones
were Mother in Heaven,
the Ancient of Nights and mother of all,
with many of her faithful daughters
who had lived through the ages.

Her Work and Glory
The work and glory
of the Mother
is to bring to pass the
immortality and
eternal life of
Her children.

The work and glory
of the Mother
is to love.

The Bearer
The Mother carried
our souls.
I asked Her,
Were they heavy?

What Margaret Taught Me
Her name means
creation itself.
Her name means
to live.

What the Mother Taught Me
Creation is
more than
procreation.
It is snow, birds,
trees, moon,
and song.

The Weaver
The Mother chooses Her
colors carefully—hope, despair,
love, fear, joy, sorrow. She
weaves the morning, weft
thread between warp, again
and again.

What Whitney Taught Me
The Mother prefers the backs
of cross-stitched canvas. She
bears testament to the beauties of
imperfection, of starts and stops, of
cross overs, of loose threads and
frayed edges.

The Great Creatress

She is the Mother of
thunder, lightning,
crocuses, children,
salt, and song.

Genesis

And God said, *Let us
make woman* in
*our image, after
our likeness.* So
God created women in
Her own image, in
the image of God
created She her;
female and male
created She them.

The Mothers of All Living

Heavenly Mother, like
Eve, means giver of life;
She of all spirits,
Eve of all bodies.
Together, they form
the soul.

The Mothering God
Birth stories often
share the same
labor words,
I cannot do this
anymore, before
She does.

The Hardest Thing
Sometimes when She looked at Her
children in the first days of creation,
the only thing She could think was,
The hardest thing I have ever done was
for you. And then she cried.

What the Mother Learned

The Mother learned how
to be always interrupted,
and tired.

The Eighth Day

On the eighth day
of creation,
the Mother rested.

Postpartum

After creation,
the Mother knew
sorrow—the emptiness
that comes after fullness,
the softness that remains
for a long time.

Choose Wisdom
The Mother
mentored Eve,
to choose Wisdom.
When she did,
the Mother
rejoiced.

Matriarchal Blessing
The Matriarch gave Her
children a blessing,
before sending them to
earth. The important
lineage and line was this.
I love you. I am your Mother.

Separation Anxiety, II

Mother, too, is anxious
when Her children cry out, a
veil of forgetting hiding Her
last words: *I will always come
back for you. It shall be
a small moment.*

Life Lesson

One of the first things
we must learn on earth
is how to sleep
without our Mother.

Silent Notes Taking

The Mother above us
notes every milestone:
first breath, first smile,
first tooth, first sit,
first crawl, first step,
first word, first prayer,
first high five, first
firefly, first faith,
first love, first break,
first doubt, first joy,
first homecoming.

What Adam Taught Me

She is not silent;
She is quiet.
To hear Her,
you must be
very still.

Still Small Voice

The Mother was not in the wind,
nor in the earthquake.
She was not in the fire,
but in a still small voice.

She Can Be Loud When She Wants

She can be in the wind.
She can be in the quake.
She can be in the fire.
She can laugh at the still small voice.

Priceless
The Mother is better than rubies,
(and pearls, and cows)
and all things that may be desired
are naught compared to Her.

Many Names
She has many names:
Sophia, Ashera, Ruah,
Thea, Korra, Luna.
She answers to them all.

Her Gifts
Her gifts are grace,
wisdom, kindness.
She shares them willingly.

A Wise Heart
The Mother is
wise in heart, and
mighty in strength.

Flesh
The Mother has a body
of flesh and bones
as tangible as women's;
Her daughters also.

The Great She Is, II

She is the God of
Sarah, Rebecca,
and Rachel.

She covenants with
Her daughters.

Tamed

The Mother became responsible
forever for what She tamed.
She is responsible for Her daughters.

The God of Your Mother

The God of your
mother will help you,
and the Almighty
will bless you
with blessings of
heaven and earth, and
breasts and womb.

The Queen

The Queen shall be
our nursing Mother.

The God Who Weeps
In heaven was there a voice heard,
lamentation, and weeping, and
great mourning, the Mother
weeping for Her children, and
would not be comforted,
because they are not.

What Chieko Taught Me
The Mother's face
is hidden from us,
because Her arms
are around us.
(Our heads rest gently
on Her shoulder.)

The One Who Watches the Sparrows
The Mother watches
Her children's mouths
curve upward, then back down—
noting the exact moment the smile
turns.

Living Waters
When the Mother
was thirsty, She
drank deeply,
from the well
of eternal life.

What Gene Taught Me

The Mother and
Father are tied
tighter than the
Godhead—the
word "God"
means both.

God So Loved the World

The Mother loved us
as much as the Father.
They sent Their Son.

The Mothers

The Mothers of
the Lord are
blessed among
women, Mary
who made room
in her body, and She
who made room
in Her spirit.

First Miracles

The Son's first miracle was
changing water into wine.
The Mother's first miracle was
changing water into milk.
She nourishes us all.

As One Whom His Mother Comforteth
She showed Her Son
how to mother, so He
could show the world.

Heavenly Parents
Heavenly Mother and
Heavenly Father are
doting parents,
saying,
Look at my Child.
Look at what my Child
can say.

Dove Tongue
The Mother spoke gently,
This is my beloved Son.
Hear Him.

Lady in the Temple
Her body
is holy
to the Lord.
It is the house
of the Lord.

When Jesus Was a Child
He said to them,
How is it that ye sought me?
Wist ye not that I must be about
my Mother's business?

Like Mother, Like Son
Christ's mission was
also to do the will
of the Mother.
He announced,
They that have seen me
have seen the Mother.

Mother Tree
After nourishing, and digging,
and pruning, and dunging,
and weeping, the Lord of the
Vineyard remembered the Mother
Tree.

He brought Her back to Her
children, then Her children
back to Her, grafting branches
into branches. Their togetherness
preserved—natural branches and roots
and the roots of their Mother Tree.
She bore good fruit.

The Good Shepherdess
She taught her Son
to call His lambs by name,
and lead them.

When she puts forth
Her own sheep,
She goes before them,
and the sheep follow Her:
for they know Her voice.

Her Voice
Her voice is a whisper—
still and deep.

- **The Bearers**
  The Mother bore
  our souls:
  Her Son,
  our grief.

He Came to Her
When the Mother
was sorrowful,
and very heavy,
She cried, *Son*.
He came to Her
from earth,
strengthening Her.

What Nathan Taught Me
He told me, *It is odd that*
with all the birthing God does—
a Son, a Holy Spirit, a creation—
that God is called 'Dad.'
Rather than a mother? I asked.
Rather than Mommy, he answered.
Instead of calling God 'Abba,'
Jesus should have called him, 'Mommy.'

In the Guise of an Angel
When Jesus
was sorrowful,
and very heavy,
He cried, *Mommy.*
She came to Him
from heaven,
strengthening Him.

Tree of Life
When Jesus was on the cross,
His Father might have been
in the farthest reaches of heaven,
for sorrow, and solace.
(We can give Him that.)
His Mother might have been
right there,
branches holding Him—
a weeping willow,
the Tree of Life.

What the Mother Carried

The Mother
carried Her Son,
as He carried
the world.

Celestial Seating

The Father sits
on the right hand
of the Mother,
alongside Their
beloved Son.

What Joseph Taught Me
If women do not comprehend
the character of God the Mother,
they do not comprehend themselves.

Mother Bear
Katie taught me
to envision Heavenly
Mother as
mother bear, fierce
and tender
for Her cubs.
(She even drew
a picture.)

What Emily Taught Me
Perfection is not Her goal,
love is.

Rainbow Mother
The Mother loves Her children fiercely,
all the red, orange, yellow, green, blue, violet,
rainbow ones.

The Mother is Tall and Wide
The Mother has
wide arms and
wide love, to
encircle all.

What Shaura Taught Me
She's here.
Like when you called home
before the time of cellphones
and your dad answered,
but you just wanted to talk
to Mom.

What Janan Taught Me
Heavenly Mother
is a black woman
with black woman
magic.

What Melody Taught Me
The Father speaks;
the Mother sings.

What Twila Taught Me
Only the ocean
comes close to
mirroring the
Mother's embrace.

The Veil
I thought the Mother
was the veil,
the ocean, kissing
earth and sky.

Saltwater
The Mother's tears
fill up the ocean—
all Her salty, sweet ones.
We can swim there,
but we cannot drink.

Stilled
The Sea is calm today.
Yesterday, She wasn't.

White Spaces
The Mother may be in
the white spaces—the
silences, sighs,
trees, and wind.

What Samuel Taught Me
The Mother is in the wind.
She moves me gently, firmly.
I feel Her force;
I see Her fruits.

Living Tree
The Mother starts her days in forests,
breathing in the deep roots,
old veins, and circle growth.
She stretches Her arms to God,
and faces light.

Tree of Life, II

When it is coldest,
She sheds her leaves,
stands bare,
vulnerable, and brave,
to let the light in.

She Covenants with Her Children
The Mother keeps Her
baptismal covenants. She
mourns when we mourn,
rejoices when we rejoice.

By Example
She taught me
how to sit with
others in their grief,
and not say
a word.

What Terry Taught Me
Our Mother's journals are blank.
We write in them.

Li-Young Lee
When I was twenty,
I heard a poet
read his poem
about God.

A girl, he said,
one of her names
is Change.

I began to cry.

When I was twenty-nine,
I read that poem
about God,
to the baby in
my womb.

A girl, I said,
one of her names
is Change.

I cried again.

Crack

The evening Cora was born,
I heard a loud crack.
It was my heart, opened.
I knew instinctively
that it would not un-crack,
and that the Mother's heart
has cracked ten billion times.

Old Eyes

I thought that when I
became a mother,
I would have new eyes,
to see the Mother.
Instead, I have old eyes,
just wise enough
to recognize Her.

God's Eyes
God's eyes are
Mother's eyes.
To see others as
God sees them,
is to see as the
Mother.

Child's Play
Heavenly Mother didn't think
She believed in toys,
until She saw her daughter
play with daylight,
wind, trees, songs.
Now she seeks to give her every
good (play)thing.

Language Acquisition

When Cora learns how to say *mommy*
will she forget how to say *Mother*?

The Linguist

The Mother reads
Her children fairytales
and philosophy books
in all the languages
of the world.

The Author

When Her children sleep,
She writes.

Maybe

Maybe it takes being a mother
to know the Mother,
to carry something inside
for months, before birthing
it into the world—
a child, a poem, an idea.

The Mother Understands
The divine
Mother
of us all,
understands
not every
woman
is a mother.

I Dreamed My Mother Was God
She had pool eyes,
and hair as wild
as mine;
a face lined with
wisdom and laughter;
a heart heavy as gold.

Her Real Name
The first thing Eden wanted to know
about Heavenly Mother was Her name.
When I told her I didn't know,
she answered her own question.
I think Heavenly Mother is Mother Nature.
One day we'll know Her real name,
like Melissa.

What the Mother Taught Me, II
To love meadows,
and walking,
and clover.

What Alicia Taught Me

Our Mother
is in the soil.
*She lives
and thrives
and dies there.*

Our Mother
is in time and light.
*She brings the following day,
the future, and the rising
of the sun.*

Earth Mother

Her breath is earthy,
soft and sweet.
Her body warm,
and nourishing.
She offers fruit and
herbs in their season;
milk and honey,
without money
and without price.

Mother Earth
Enoch heard Her voice
from Her deep places.
Wo, wo is me,
the Mother of women;
I am pained, I am weary.
When shall I rest?
And when Enoch
heard Her mourn,
he mourned, too.

A Reverse of Birth
Mother Earth holds us
first on Her lap,
then in Her womb.

Our bodies become
one with the body
of our Mother.
New life
out of death again.

The Morning Søren Was Born
I heard the Mother's
birth cries
from my
own
mouth.

A State of Rest
The Mother isn't
tired anymore.
She sleeps when
Her children sleep,
dreams when
they dream.

The Nourishing

The Spirit of Eliza
Eliza the Prophetess
came, and turned
the heart of the Mother
to Her children,
and the hearts of the children
to their Mother.

The First Order of Business
She said,
Be still,
and know
that I am
God.

Wild Rumpus
She is now the Queen,
and She will be a truly great Queen.

Family Resemblance
The Mother searches for Her
features in Her daughter's face,
anything that bears Her relation.
Then She sees it:
the shape of a line here,
a spark of kindness there.

A Fire is Burning
Sometimes the desire to feel
close to Her is its own warmth.
Sometimes it is enough.

I've a Mother There
Eliza knew it from reason.
I know it from a feeling
and a hope.

I've a Mother Here
She is close.
She is kind.
She cares.

In Which the Potter Imprints Herself
The Mother holds the clay
and shapes it,
resting only when
each vessel resembles
God.

Before
Before She formed
me in the belly,
She knew me.

From the Womb
Before I was born,
I heard Her.

Mother Tongue, II
She gave me
Her language,
in the womb.

First Friend
When I was a spirit girl,
I lived with God.
I was Her companion,
and She mine.

What Claudia Taught Me
What a womb is,
and how a
Mother's love
encircles.

Motherland
She is my motherland—
the place where I was born.

The Most Repeated Truths
We are loved by Her.
We are to become like Her.

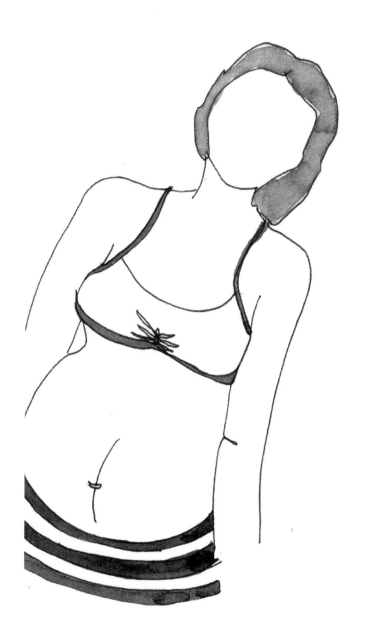

Milk and Honey

My hunger makes Her
breasts let down, soaking Her
shirt with milk and honey.

My Mama Answers Me

I root, open-mouthed
and howling.
She answers,
nursing me
on demand.

Perfect Blessing

The Mother held
me in her arms
and blessed me,
giving me
my name.

Tamed, II
She and I are tied together
in a way I cannot explain.

Communion
The Mother offered me
Her breast, saying,
This is My body.
Take.
Eat.

Mother's Milk
Her milk is made
for each child,
as individual
as it is infinite.
She knows our
needs by kissing.

She Soothed Me
When I awoke to Her absence
She soothed me.
You woke up and
your Mommy was gone,
That must have been
so scary.

She Kissed Me

Before my Mother
left the room,
She kissed me
gently, and said,
I am coming right back.
I am close.
After my Mother
entered the room,
She kissed me
gently, and said,
I did not forget you.

God Remembered Rachel

The Mother cannot forget
Her sucking child;
She has compassion on
the daughter of Her womb.

Our Hunger
Our hunger
interrupts
Her dreams,
and is the
reason She
remembers
them.

When the Bough Breaks
Rock-a-bye
babe. When the
wind blows,
cradle rocks,
bough breaks,
cradle falls,
your Mommy
will catch you.

Maybe Her Name is Beatrice
She holds my hand
and guides me
into all truth.

The Very Hairs of Your Head
The Mother is forever brushing
Her child's hair behind her ears.

Breakfast
The Mother loves
them that love Her;
and those that seek Her
early shall find Her.
(We will dine for breakfast.)

In God's House

The front door
is wide open,
the porch full—
Mother and Father
sipping lemonade,
reading books aloud
to every child.

Sunday Mornings
I try on my
Mother's shoes/
necklace/earrings as
She smiles.

Mother/Daughter Date
She takes me
for frozen yogurt
on bad days.

Are You My Mother, II
When the bird was young,
she called everyone *Mother*.
When the bird was young,
She said, *Here I am*.

Birdie
She left me
in our nest,
returned with
sustenance and
song, before
urging me
to fly.

Mama Bird
The Mother still remembers to sing
every morning and night—
lullabies for her children.

She Remembers Everything
Every hair.
Every little bird.

Mother Hen
Oft the Mother gathers me
as a hen gathereth her chickens
under her wings,
and nourishes me.

· **She Came To Her**
When the daughter
was sorrowful,
and very heavy,
she cried, *Mommy*.
She came to her
from heaven,
strengthening her.

Tree of Life, III
The Mother is a
home, for every
being who flies.

Salt and Light
We are the salt
of the Mother's earth.
We are the light
set on Her hill.

Bread of Life
The Mother rises,
and falls,
and rises,
giving life
to the whole
world.

Body Memory

Does it matter
that Her body
remembers
the pangs of
menstruation,
infertility, and
childbirth?
(It does to me.)

Her Repertoire

She knows the song the
morning stars sang
together, and the one the
mourning stars sang by
themselves.

She sang it first—the
melody of grief, with its
accompaniment of pain, the
breve and quaver rests, both
bereaving and quivering, the
fermata, firmly holding on to
what was lost, the
tremolo of mourning
sickness.

What Janice Taught Me

She is always
with mothers
as they form
bodies.

Heavenly Doula

God's Spirit, God's Breath,
the one He could not live without,
gave me breath when I
gave my daughter life.

She sat beside me on the precipice,
so I would not be alone. We exhaled
and inhaled in unison. She whispered,
calling me by name.

Intuition
She laughs just before I laugh,
weeps before I weep,
hungers before I hunger.
Our spirits are one,
though they look like two.
Her milk keeps me alive.

Yawn
I yawned wide enough to birth Cora.
The Mother yawned as wide as eternity.
And all eternity shook.

Ears to Hear

The Father could not hear
His daughter's whimpering,
though He slept beside her
in the same room.
The Mother woke at every sound.

Ears to Hear, II

The Mother can distinguish
Her daughter's cries:
hunger, fatigue, *leave me be*,
loneliness, boredom, anger,
sorrow, uncleanliness.
She attends each one.

Lifting With Our Knees

On hard days I cannot carry my child's cries;
her tears are too heavy, the weight too awkward.
My Mother comes ready to the other side.
We lift together, with our knees.

Midnight Bike Rides
I biked each month under the full moon
to the place where land and water meet.
Now I turn my child to my Mother's care
at night, and thank the lady of the light.

Lunar Light
When the night fell, I found Her
smiling at the earth, casting
Her gentle glow upon it,
Her love directing waves and women;
each connected to the moon.

Mirror Image

It is difficult to say now
if She was created in
my image, or I in Hers.
What is easy to say now is
when I look inside a mirror,
I see God.

Darkly

I look through
the glass, darkly,
and can just barely
make Her out.

Crack, II
Something cracked open.
She is everywhere.

For a Moment
When I was tired,
I hid my face
from Cora.
The Mother
hid not her face
from me.

Veil
When my daughter cried
for me as I showered,
I gave her soft words.
I'm right here.
I'm just on the other side
of the curtain.
And suddenly,
I knew my Mother
was.

The Mother is Not Absent
She is taking
a long shower,
a nap, and using
the bathroom
by Herself.

The Comforter
Cora's word for *comfort*
is *Mama*.

Close to a Miracle
A baby's ability
to recognize
his Mother
is everything.

After Sleeping in the Forest
Mary wrote,
I thought the earth
remembered me,
she took me back
so tenderly.
I thought the
same thing of
my Mother.
I thought, *Amen.*

Recognition
Chris dreamt
she saw the Mother
in a grove of trees.
When She turned around;
she knew Her face.

I am Close

When Søren was born,
I found myself repeating
Mother words:
I did not forget you. It will be
a small moment.
I am close, I am close,
I am close.

Homecoming

The Mother felt Her daughter
ecstatic, catapulting against
Her, *I never thought*
I'd see you again!
Why?
I don't know why.

My Daughter Talks to God

C:
*I'm sad because
I was lonely. I called
Mommy, Mommy,
Mommy.*

She:
*That's why
I'm here.
You called and
I came.*

What Jeffrey Taught Me
The Mother
reaches across
vast desert-
scapes
to find us.

The Mother Delights in Plainness
She speaks to
us in ways we
understand.

Sound Memory
I hear Her in every
good sound—
Cora's laugh,
bird songs,
popped acorns,
wind rush,
bells, violin
strings, pianos,
rustling leaves,
fireworks, "oohs"
and "ahs."

What Jim Taught Me
To hear my
Mother's voice
gently calling, and
the sound of love
and wisdom
fills my ear.

A Planet and a Star
What makes the heavens beautiful
is that somewhere they hold the Mother.

My First Article of Faith
I believe in God the Eternal
Father and Mother,
and in their Son, Jesus Christ,
and in the Holy Ghost.

My Second
I am a daughter
of Heavenly Parents,
who love me,
and I love Them.

Re-turned

When I turned my
heart to my Mother,
Her heart turned
toward me.

I Always Do

When I was afraid of
the dark in my room,
my Mother asked,
*Do you feel safe when
you're with Me?*
I answered,
I always do.

What J.P. Taught Me

She's a *nightlight
for us people,
sent down here
to earth.*

What Calvin Taught Me

*Home is where
your Mother is.*

As She Is
When She shall appear
we shall be like Her,
for we shall see Her
as She is.

Pink Moccasins
I saw Her, in
Her own house,
wearing pink
moccasins
and speaking
as loud
as humanly
possible.

Mother-full

The Mother is in
my library, re-
collected by my
sister poets,
Eliza, Carol Lynn,
Joanna,
Lisa, Margaret,
Melody.
She is in my sisters,
Cumorah, Liahona,
Charity.
She is in my mother,
Claudia.

Mine is a Mother-
full house.
I can live here.

Giants
I stand on the
shoulders of
giant-souled
writers, who shared
their Mother
hunger/reaching/
learning/nourishing
first.

I bless them.

What Joanna Taught Me
*God is a Mother and
a Father.*
I matter. I matter.
I matter.

Holy Places
We climbed to
the mountain top,
She and I,
and sat awhile.

The Law of Adoption
The Mother and I
adopted each other,
binding ourselves
to the whole imperfect
frayed, tangled,
beautiful, human,
Godly family.

Eternal Life
This is life eternal:
to know Her.

Olive Wood
The Mother shares
fresh oil and
new wine—
anointing,
giving light.

The Dwelling
Her body is
still my home.
I fall asleep,
on Her mountain
chest.

Mother Who Knows
The Mother knows
we have need
of all these things.

The Truth

The truth is, I can't stop
searching for my Mother.
The truth is, I don't know if
She wants to be found. But
something big and tiny in
my heart tells me that She
does—that She too, like
Her children, wants
to be seen.

What Moana Taught Me

The Mother's heart
can be stolen, but
it can also be
restored.

Conch-shells

They are not the ocean;
they are memories of the ocean.
Birds. Trees. Olive oil. Bread. Moons.
They are not the Mother;
they are memories of the Mother.
I hear Her everywhere.

Benediction
Dear God,
May the Mother
long for me
as I long for Her,
may She run to me,
as I run to Her,
may She soothe me,
as I soothe
my son
and daughter.
In Jesus' name,
Amen.

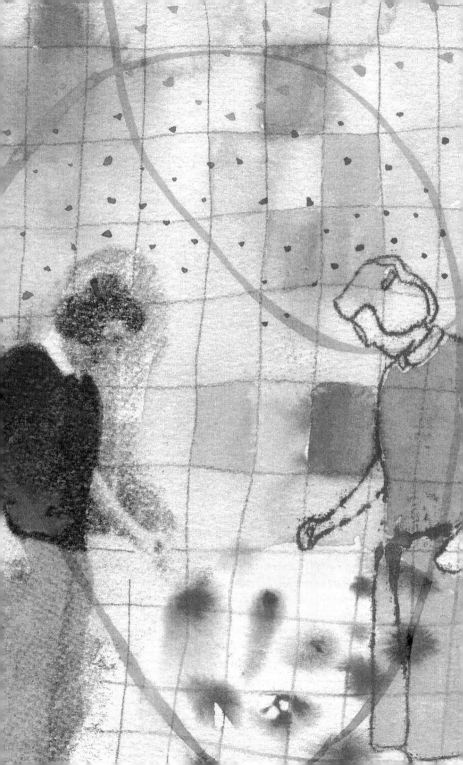

Notes

Motherless Milk   Title via Annie K. Blake. Inspired (as so many of my poems are), by Cora. Also inspired by Søren Kierkegaard's *Exordium* in *Fear and Trembling* (Princeton: Princeton University Press, 1983).

I. "When the child is to be weaned, the mother blackens her breast. It would be hard to have the breast look inviting when the child must not have it. So the child believes that the breast has changed, but the mother—she is still the same, her gaze is tender and loving as ever. How fortunate the one who did not need more terrible means to wean the child!" 11.

II. "When the child has grown big and is to be weaned, the mother virginally conceals her breast, and then the child no longer has a mother. How fortunate the child who has not lost his mother in some other way!" 12.

IV. "When the child is to be weaned, the mother has stronger sustenance at hand so that the child does not perish. How fortunate the one who has this stronger sustenance at hand." 14.

What Søren Aabye Taught Me   Søren Kierkegaard, *Exordium* III. "When the child is to be weaned, the mother, too, is not without sorrow, because she and the child are more and more to be separated, because the child who first lay under her heart and later rested upon her breast will never again be so close. So they grieve together the brief sorrow. How fortunate the one who kept the child so close and did not need to grieve any more!" in *Fear and Trembling* (Princeton: Princeton University Press, 1983), 13.

The Very Hungry Girl   Inspired by Eric Carle's *The Very Hungry Caterpillar* (New York: Philomel Books, 1981).

Story Time   Inspired by Stephin Merritt, "The Book of Love," The Magnetic Fields, *69 Love Songs* (Merge Records, 1999). "I love it when you read to me. And you, you can read me anything."

Lost Boys   J.M. Barrie, *Peter Pan* (New York: Atheneum Books for Young Readers, 2014).

Lost Girl   J.M. Barrie, *Peter Pan* (New York: Atheneum Books for Young Readers, 2014).

What Carol Taught Me   Carol P. Christ, "Why Women Need the Goddess," *Heresies* 2.1 *The Great Goddess* (1978), 8–13. "Religious symbol systems focused around exclusively male images of divinity create the impression that female power can never be fully legitimate or wholly beneficent . . . A woman . . . may see herself as like God (created in the image of God) only by denying her own sexual identity and affirming God's transcendence of sexual identity. But she can never have the experience that is freely available to every man and boy in her culture, of having her full sexual identity affirmed as being in the image and likeness of God."

. . .

A second important implication of the Goddess symbol for women is the affirmation of the female body and the life cycle expressed in it. Because of women's unique position as menstruants, birth-givers, and those who have traditionally cared for the young and the dying, women's connection to the body, nature, and this world has been obvious. Women were denigrated because they seemed more carnal, fleshy, and earthy than the culture-creating males.

Lost Lady   Margaret Barker, via her presentation at "The Worlds of Joseph Smith: A Bicentennial Conference at the Library of Congress": "… she was Wisdom, the one whom Josiah eventually purged from the temple, but whose symbol, the Tree of Life, had been removed many years earlier, in the time of Isaiah, and then replaced. In the time of Josiah, her tree, the Asherah, the Menorah, was finally removed from the temple." Then, "There were long memories of the lost temple. In the time of the Messiah, it was said, the true temple would be restored and all missing things would be put back: the spirit, the fire, the cherubim, and the ark, but also the anointing oil and the menorah." Transcribed by Joe Hunt, http://www.joehunt .org/joseph-smith-margaret-barker-talk.html.

Amiri   From Amiri Baraka's poem, "Preface to a Twenty Volume Suicide Note." "And now, each night I count the stars, And each night I get the same number. And when they will not come to be counted, I count the holes they leave," in LeRoi Jones' *Preface to a Twenty Volume Suicide Note....* (New York: Totem Press/Corinth Books, 1961), 5. For Charity.

What Rosemary Taught Me   Rosemary Radford Ruether, *Sexism and God-talk: Toward a Feminist Theology* (Boston: Beacon Press, 1993).

Unmothered   Title inspired both by Meghan O'Rourke's "Unmothered, on Mother's Day," *Slate*, May 6, 2010, http://www.slate.com/articles/life/grieving/2010/05/unmothered_on_mothers_day.html and Ruth Margalit's "The Unmothered," *The New Yorker,* May 9, 2014. http://www.newyorker.com/books/page-turner/the-unmothered.

First Grief   Title inspired by Margaret Rampton Munk's poem, "First Grief," *Exponent II* 5.1 (1978), 17.

Every Day   Inspired by Meghan O'Rourke: *"Unmothered* is not a word in the dictionary, but, I often find myself thinking it should be. The 'real' word most like it—it never escapes me—is *unmoored*. The irreplaceability is what becomes stronger—and stranger—as the months pass: Am I really she who has woken up again without a mother? Yes, I am." "Unmothered, on Mother's Day," *Slate*, May 6, 2010, http://www.slate.com/articles/life/grieving/2010/05/unmothered_on_mothers_day.html.

Looking For My Mother Proverbs 8:1; 10 "Doth not wisdom cry? and understanding put forth her voice?... Receive my instruction, and not silver; and knowledge rather than choice gold."

The Woman in the Wilderness Revelation 12:6 "And the woman fled into the wilderness, where she hath a place prepared of God..."

The Woman in the Moon Joe Hunt.

Are You My Mother? Inspired by P.D. Eastman's children's book, *Are You My Mother?* (New York: Random House for Young Readers, 1998).

Non-fiction Lisa van Orman Hadley, "Irreversible Things," *Epoch,* 63.2 (2014).

Are You There, God Judy Blume, *Are You There God? It's Me, Margaret.* (New York: Atheneium Books for Young Readers, 2014).

Breathe Inspired by Friedrich Nietzsche: "God is dead. God remains dead. And we have killed him." *The Gay Science* (New York: Cambridge University Press, 2001), 120.

Follow Your Nose Title inspired by 1980s era Kellogg's Froot Loop commercials.

The Hour She Learned She Was God   John 16:21 "A woman when she is in travail hath sorrow, because her hour is come: but as soon as she is delivered of the child, she remembereth no more the anguish, for joy that a man is born into the world."

The Great She Is   Exodus 3:14 "And God said unto Moses, I AM THAT I AM: and he said, Thus shalt thou say unto the children of Israel, I AM hath sent me unto you."

In the Beginning   Genesis 1:3 "And God said, Let there be light: and there was light." Plus, wisdom from Kristine Haglund.

She Laid the Measures Thereof   Job 38:5–7 "Who hath laid the measures thereof, if thou knowest? or who hath stretched the line upon it? Whereupon are the foundations thereof fastened? or who laid the corner stone thereof; When the morning stars sang together, and all the sons of God shouted for joy?"

Luna   For Luna.

Ancient of Nights   D&C 138:38–39 "Among the great and mighty ones who were assembled in this vast congregation of the righteous were Father Adam, the Ancient of Days and father of all, And our glorious Mother Eve, with many of her faithful daughters who had lived through the ages and worshiped the true and living God."

Her Work and Glory   Moses 1:39 "For behold, this is my work and my glory—to bring to pass the immortality and eternal life of man."

What Margaret Taught Me   Margaret Toscano: "'John A. Phillips says . . . We cannot understand the history of Eve without seeing her as a deposed Creator-Goddess, and indeed, in some sense as creation itself.' In actuality Eve's name is not taken from the verb 'to be' but is derived from a Hebrew root (*chaya*) which means 'to live.'" "Put on Your Strength O Daughters of Zion: Claiming Priesthood and Knowing the Mother," in *Women and Authority,* ed. Maxine Hanks (Salt Lake City: Signature Books, 1992), 428.

The Weaver   Inspired by Carol Lynn Pearson's play *Mother Wove the Morning* (Walnut Creek, CA: Pearson, 1995) and Whitney Bushman's photograph, *Untitled* (September 12, 2002), exhibited in *Immediate Present,* curated by Laura Allred Hurtado at New York City's Riverside Church for the inaugural Mormon Arts Center Festival, and my own response "We Have Need of Each Other," published in the accompanying catalog, *Immediate Present* (New York: Mormon Arts Center, 2017).

What Whitney Taught Me   Similarly inspired by Whitney Bushman's untitled artwork and my response "We Have Need of Each Other," *Immediate Present* (New York: Mormon Arts Center, 2017).

The Great Creatress   Title inspired by Margaret Toscano: "The 'Mother of All Living,' is the title given anciently to may goddesses, but it was principally ascribed to the Creatress." "Put on Your Strength O Daughters of Zion: Claiming Priesthood and Knowing the Mother," in *Women and Authority,* ed. Maxine Hanks (Salt Lake City: Signature Books, 1992), 428.

Genesis   Genesis 1:27 "So God created man in his own image, in the image of God created he him; male and female created he them."

The Mothers of All Living   Genesis 3:20 "And Adam called his wife's name Eve; because she was the mother of all living."

The Mothering God   Jason Kerr, "The Image of the Mothering God," *By Common Consent* blog, May 8, 2016, https://bycommonconsent.com/2016/05/08/the-image-of-the-mothering-god/. "Lauren Winner draws on a friend's observation that nearly every birth story includes a moment when the laboring woman says, 'I cannot do this anymore.'"

Separation Anxiety, II   D&C 121:7–8 "My son, peace be unto thy soul; thine adversity and thine afflictions shall be but a small moment. And then, if thou endure it well, God shall exalt thee on high; thou shalt triumph over all thy foes."

Silent Notes Taking   Title from hymn, "Do What is Right," text by Anon., The Psalms of Life, Boston, 1857, Hymnal (Salt Lake City, UT: The Church of Jesus Christ of Latter-day Saints, 1985), 237.

What Adam Taught Me   Adam Miller, *Letters to a Young Mormon,* Maxwell Institute, 2013, 40. "You may discover that God's silence is not itself a rebuke but an invitation. The heaven's aren't empty, they're quiet. And God, rather than turning you away, may be inviting you to share this silence with him."

Still Small Voice   1 Kings 19:11–12 "And he said, Go forth, and stand upon the mount before the Lord. And, behold, the Lord passed by, and a great and strong wind rent the mountains, and brake in pieces the rocks before the Lord; but the Lord was not in the wind: and after the wind an earthquake; but the Lord was not in the earthquake: And after the earthquake a fire; but the Lord was not in the fire: and after the fire a still small voice."

Priceless   Proverbs 8:11 "For wisdom is better than rubies; and all the things that may be desired are not to be compared to it."

Many Names   Additional names could have been added, including Hokmah and Shekinah. For Thea, and Cora, and Luna.

Flesh   D&C 130:23 "The Father has a body of flesh and bones as tangible as man's; the Son also ... "

The Great She Is, II   Exodus 3:6 "Moreover he said, I am the God of thy father, the God of Abraham, the God of Isaac, and the God of Jacob..."

Tamed   Antoine de Saint-Exupéry, *The Little Prince*, trans. by Richard Howard. "'People have forgotten this truth,' the fox said. 'But you mustn't forget it. You become responsible forever for what you've tamed. You're responsible for your rose.'" (New York: Houghton Mifflin Harcourt, 2000) 68.

The God of Your Mother   Genesis 49:25 "Even by the God of thy father, who shall help thee; and by the Almighty, who shall bless thee with blessings of heaven above, blessings of the deep that lieth under, blessings of the breasts, and of the womb."

The Queen   Isaiah 49:23 "And kings shall be thy nursing fathers, and their queens thy nursing mothers: they shall bow down to thee with their face toward the earth, and lick up the dust of thy feet; and thou shalt know that I am the Lord: for they shall not be ashamed that wait for me."

The God Who Weeps   Title from Fiona and Terryl Givens book, *The God Who Weeps: How Mormonism Makes Sense of Life* (Salt Lake City, UT: Deseret Book, 2012). And, Matthew 2:18 "In Rama was there a voice heard, lamentation, and weeping, and great mourning, Rachel weeping for her children, and would not be comforted, because they are not."

What Chieko Taught Me   Chieko Okazaki: "The gospel teaches us that each individual is a precious and cherished child of heavenly parents." "A Living Network," *Ensign* (1995). And: "Heavenly Father stands with us in our most anguished moments. He knows what we are thinking and feeling. Though his face is hidden from us, his arms are around us." *Sanctuary* (Salt Lake City, UT: Deseret Book, 1997), 149.

The One Who Watches the Sparrows   Luke 12:6–7 "Are not five sparrows sold for two farthings, and not one of them is forgotten before God? But even the very hairs of your head are all numbered. Fear not therefore: ye are of more value than many sparrows."

Living Waters   John 4:13–14 "Jesus answered and said unto her, Whosoever drinketh of this water shall thirst again: But whosoever drinketh of the water that I shall give him shall never thirst; but the water that I shall give him shall be in him a well of water springing up into everlasting life."

What Gene Taught Me   Eugene England: "Modern scriptures and revelations suggest quite plainly that we would more accurately and profitably read the scriptural references to 'God' as meaning God the eternal partnership of Heavenly Father and Heavenly Mother. They have a more perfect unity even than that of God and Christ and the Holy Ghost, and so the word God implies both of them, at least as much as it denotes the three beings in the classical Christian trinity called 'God.'" "Becoming Bone of Bone and Flesh of Flesh," in *As Women of*

Faith: Talks Selected from the BYU Women's Conferences, ed. Mary E. Stovall and Carol Cornwall Madsen (Salt Lake City, UT: Deseret Book, 1989), 110.

(Erastus Snow agreed: "Now, it is not said in so many words in the Scriptures, that we have a Mother in heaven as well as a Father. It is left for us to infer this from what we see and know of all living things in the earth including man. The male and female principle is united and both necessary to the accomplishment of the object of their being, and if this be not the case with our Father in heaven after whose image we are created, then it is an anomaly in nature. But to our minds the idea of a Father suggests that of a Mother.... Hence when it is said that God created our first parents in His likeness... it is intimated in language sufficiently plain to my understanding that the male and female principle was present with the Gods as it is with man." *Journal of Discourses*, 26:214 (1855).)

God So Loved the World   John 3:16 "For God so loved the world, that he gave his only begotten Son, that whosoever believeth in him should not perish, but have everlasting life."

The Mothers   Luke 1:41–42 "And it came to pass, that, when Elisabeth heard the salutation of Mary, the babe leaped in her womb; and Elisabeth was filled with the Holy Ghost: And she spake out with a loud voice, and said, Blessed art thou among women, and blessed is the fruit of thy womb."

First Miracles   John 2:1–11: "And the third day there was a marriage in Cana of Galilee; and the mother of Jesus was there: And both Jesus was called, and his disciples, to the marriage. And when they wanted wine, the mother of Jesus saith unto him, They have no wine. Jesus saith unto her, Woman, what have I to do with thee? mine hour is not yet come. His mother saith unto the servants, Whatsoever he saith unto you do it. And there were set there six waterpots of stone, after the manner of the purifying of the Jews, containing two or three firkins apiece. Jesus saith unto them, Fill the waterpots with water. And they filled them up to the brim. And he saith unto them, Draw out now, and bear unto the governor of the feast. And they bare it. When the ruler of the feast had tasted the water that was made wine, and knew not whence it was: (but the servants which drew the water knew;) the governor of the feast called the bridegroom, and saith unto him, Every man at the beginning doth set forth good wine; and when men have well drunk, then that which is worse: but thou hast kept the good wine until now. This beginning of miracles did Jesus in Cana of Galilee, and manifested forth his glory; and his disciples believed on him."

As One Whom His Mother Comforteth   Isaiah 66:12–13 "For thus saith the Lord, Behold, I will extend peace to her like a river, and the glory of the Gentiles like a flowing stream: then shall ye suck, ye shall be borne upon her sides, and be dandled upon her knees. As one whom his mother comforteth, so will I comfort you; and ye shall be comforted in Jerusalem."

Heavenly Parents Joseph Smith—History 1:17 "... I saw two Personages, whose brightness and glory defy all description, standing above me in the air. One of them spake unto me, calling me by name and said, pointing to the other—*This is My Beloved Son. Hear Him!*"

Dove Tongue JST, Matthew 3:45-46 "And Jesus when he was baptized, went up straightway out of the water; *and John saw,* and lo, the heavens were opened unto him, and he saw the Spirit of God descending like a dove and lighting upon *Jesus.* And lo, *he heard* a voice from heaven, saying, This is my beloved Son, in whom I am well pleased. *Hear ye him.*"

Lady in the Temple "Holiness to the Lord. The house of the Lord."

When Jesus Was a Child Luke 2:49 "And he said unto them, How is it that ye sought me? Wist ye not that I must be about my Father's business?" via wisdom from Melody Newey Johnson.

Like Mother, Like Son John 14:9 "Jesus saith unto him, Have I been so long time with you, and yet has thou not known me, Philip? he that hath seen me hath seen the Father; and how sayest thou then, Shew us the Father?"

Mother Tree Inspired by Amber Richardson and her insights on Jacob 5. "As I've studied the Mother Tree at the center of that parable I've been given perspective and peace. The fruit of the Mother Tree only goes bad when the branches are 'lofty' and outgrow the roots, but so long as the branches grow in tandem with the roots, the tree produces good fruit. When I think of myself as a natural branch of that Mother Tree I am deeply comforted by the final reunion of the two. Isn't it so beautiful that the goal of the Lord of the Vineyard is always to return the branch to the Mother? As offspring of a Divine Mother it truly is natural for us to desire and one day realize this grafting process, this reunion, and when we allow the gardener, our Lord Jesus Christ, to guide us through it we will find that our roots and branches, our hearts and minds, will grow equivalently until we are ready for Her to reveal Herself to us." Amber Richardson's Facebook page, accessed June 2017. (Shared with permission.)

Jacob 5:54–56, 60 "And, behold, the roots of the natural branches of the tree which I planted whithersoever I would are yet alive; wherefore, that I may preserve them also for mine own purpose, I will take of the branches of this tree, and I will graft them in unto them. Yea, I will graft in unto them the branches of their mother tree, that I may preserve the roots also unto mine own self, that when they shall be sufficiently strong perhaps they may bring forth good fruit unto me, and I may yet have glory in the fruit of my vineyard. And it came to pass that they took from the natural tree which had become wild, and grafted in unto the natural trees, which also had become wild. And they also took of the natural trees which had become wild, and grafted into their mother tree. And because that I have preserved the natural branches and the roots thereof, and that I have grafted in the natural branches again into their mother tree, and have preserved the roots of their mother tree, that, perhaps, the trees of my vineyard may bring forth again good fruit; and that I may have joy again in the fruit of my vineyard, and, perhaps, that I may rejoice exceedingly that I have preserved the roots and the branches of the first fruit."

The Good Shepherdess   John 10:3–4 "... and he calleth his own sheep by name, and leadeth them out. And when he putteth forth his own sheep, he goeth before them, and the sheep follow him: for they know his voice."

Her Voice   Søren Kierkegaard, "[T]he voice of God is always a whisper ... " *Two Ages: "The Age of Revolution" and "The Present Age" A Literary Review* (Princeton: Princeton University Press, 2009), 10. And, "When the ocean is exerting all its power, that is precisely the time when it cannot reflect the image of heaven, and even the slightest motion blurs the image; but when it becomes still and deep, then the image of heaven sinks into its nothingness." *Eighteen Upbuilding Discourses* (Princeton: Princeton University Press, 1992), 299.

He Came to Her   Matthew 26:37 "And he took with him Peter and the two sons of Zebedee, and began to be sorrowful and very heavy." Luke 22:43 "And there appeared an angel unto him from heaven, strengthening him."

In the Guise of an Angel   Matthew 26:37 "And he took with him Peter and the two sons of Zebedee, and began to be sorrowful and very heavy." Luke 22:41–44 "And he was withdrawn from them about a stone's cast, and kneeled down, and prayed, Saying, Father, if thou be willing, remove this cup from me: nevertheless not my will, but thine, be done. And there appeared an angel unto him from heaven, strengthening him. And being in an agony he prayed more earnestly: and his sweat was as it were great drops of blood falling down to the ground."

Tree of Life   Melvin J. Ballard, "In that hour I think I can see our dear Father, behind the veil looking upon these dying struggles until even he could not endure it any longer, and, like the mother who bids farewell to her dying child, has to be taken out of the room, so as not to look upon the last struggles, so he bowed his head, and hid in some part of his universe, his great heart almost breaking for the love that he had for his Son." "His Great Heart Almost Breaking," http://emp.byui.edu/huffr/ His%20Great%20Heart%20Almost%20Breaking%20--%20 Melvin%20J.%20Ballard.htm.

Chieko Okazaki, "I wonder at the strength and courage of our Heavenly Parents, sending us to experience mortality, and of all the deaths they have suffered through with us in our own suffering. We know something of the Father's powerful grief as he withdrew from his Son, Jesus Christ, as Christ fulfilled the Atonement and died on the cross." "Walking through the

Valley of the Shadow," in *Sanctuary* (Salt Lake City, UT: Deseret Book, 1997), 148–149.

Celestial Seating   D&C 20:24 "And ascended into heaven, to sit down on the right hand of the Father, to reign with almighty power according to the will of the Father."

What Joseph Taught Me   Joseph Smith: "If men do not comprehend the character of God, they do not comprehend themselves." "The King Follett Sermon," republished in *The Ensign,* April 1971.

The Mother is Tall and Wide   Title via Annie K. Blake. 2 Nephi 1:15 "But behold, the Lord hath redeemed my soul from hell; I have beheld his glory, and I am encircled about eternally in the arms of his love."

What Janan Taught Me   Janan Graham-Russell, "Heavenly Mother is a Black Woman," *By Common Consent* blog, April 23, 2017, https://bycommonconsent.com/2017/04/23/heavenly-mother-is-a -black-woman-exploring-a-mormon-womanism/.

What Samuel Taught Me   Samuel M. Brown, *First Principles and Ordinances: The Fourth Article of Faith in Light of the Temple* (Provo, UT: Maxwell Institute, 2014), 111–112. "Pneuma comes from a word meaning 'wind' or breath,' much as the Hebrew word *ruach.* For early Christians, the word *pneuma* represented a way to express at least two key concepts. First is the close association between our breath and our lives. To live is to breathe, to breathe is to live. At the moment when we die, a moment our ancestors knew all too well, our breath dissipates as our chest stills. It is natural to connect breath and the spark of life, not least because breathing is the activity that distinguishes a sleeping body from a corpse. Second is the image of the wind, something powerful that is visible only by its effects. Pneuma subsequently carried with it a sense of invisible efficacy. Wind cannot be seen directly, but its awesome effects are easily witnessed; the same is true of the power or influence of god. When we breathe, we draw into and expel from our bodies the wind that circulates around us." Thanks to Ardis Parshall for helping me (re)find the source.

She Covenants with Her Children Mosiah 18:8–9 "And it came to pass that he said unto them: Behold, here are the waters of Mormon (for thus were they called) and now, as ye are desirous to come into the fold of God, and to be called his people, and are willing to bear one another's burdens, that they may be light; Yeah, and are willing to mourn with those that mourn; yea, and comfort those that stand in need of comfort . . . " Romans 12:15 "Rejoice with them that do rejoice, and weep with them that weep."

What Terry Taught Me Terry Tempest Williams, *When Women Were Birds: Fifty-four Variations on Voice.* "They were exactly where she said they would be: three shelves of beautiful cloth-bound books. . . . I opened the first journal. It was empty.

I opened the second journal. It was empty. I opened the third. It too was empty, as was the fourth, the fifth, the sixth—shelf after shelf after shelf, all of my mother's journals were blank" (New York: Picador, 2013), 2.

Li-Young Lee   Li-Young Lee's poem, "Living with Her," read at a Brigham Young University forum in Provo, UT, Fall 2003, in his speech "Infinite Inwardness," https://speeches.byu.edu/talks/li -young-lee_infinite-inwardness/.

I Dreamed My Mother Was God   Title inspired from Paul Auster's national story project, *I Thought My Father Was God: And Other True Tales,* (New York: Picador, 2002).

What the Mother Taught Me, II   Phyllis Luch, "O mother, I give you my love with each flower, to give forth sweet fragrance a whole lifetime through; for if I love blossoms and meadows and walking, I learn how to love them, dear mother, from you." "I Often Go Walking," *Children's Songbook* (Salt Lake City, UT: Church of Jesus Christ of Latter-day Saints, 1989), 202. For Claudia Hunt.

What Alicia Taught Me   Alicia Harris, "We are asked to care for and till the earth, and we are blessed when we have a garden. I find the idea of stewardship a unique facet in the theology of Mormonism. God the Mother is in the garden. She lives and thrives and dies there. She is smoldering under the rocks. An astrophysicist once told me that the way in which a pendulum swings (its velocity and arc) reveals the pulse of the planet.

Her pulse." "Earth Mother, Part II," *The Exponent* blog, May 19, 2014, http://www.the-exponent.com/earth-mother-part-ii/.

"The earth teaches us about feminine time, about dying and about living. The earth's time is cyclical and carries us through our hard parts. The earth knows when it's time to let things die, and then they do. And the earth also knows how to bing things back to life and make them whole again. In that ceremony last year, a blessing was invoked from a Grandmother, who is believed to live in the East. She brings the following day, the future, and the rising of the sun every day." "Earth Mother, Part I," *The Exponent* blog, May 16, 2014, http://www.the-exponent.com/earth-mother-part-i/.

Mother Earth   Moses 7:48–49 "And it came to pass that Enoch looked upon the earth; and he heard a voice from the bowels thereof, saying: Wo, wo is me, the mother of men; I am pained, I am weary, because of the wickedness of my children. When shall I rest, and be cleansed from the filthiness which is gone forth out of me? When will my Creator sanctify me, that I may rest, and righteousness for a season abide upon my face? And when Enoch heard the earth mourn, he wept, and cried unto the Lord, saying: O Lord, wilt thou not have compassion on the earth? Wilt thou not bless the children of Noah?"

The Spirit of Eliza   Malachi 4: 5–6 "Behold, I will send you Elijah the prophet before the coming of the great and dreadful day of the Lord: And he shall turn the heart of the fathers to the children, and the heart of the children to their fathers..."

The First Order of Business   Inspired by Maurice Sendak's, *Where the Wild Things Are* (New York: HarperCollins, 1984). "And when he came to the place where the wild things are they roared their terrible roars and gnashed their terrible teeth and rolled their terrible eyes and showed their terrible claws til Max said, 'BE STILL!'" Also inspired by Psalm 46:10 "Be still, and know that I am God..."

Wild Rumpus   Maurice Sendak, *Where the Wild Things Are* (New York: HarperCollins, 1984). "[T]hey called him the most wild thing of all and made him king of all wild things."

A Fire is Burning   Title from William W. Phelps hymn, "The Spirit of God," *Hymnal* (Salt Lake City, UT: The Church of Jesus Christ of Latter-day Saints, 1985), 2.

I've a Mother There   Eliza R. Snow, "O My Father." "In the heav'ns are parents single? No, the thought makes reason stare! Truth is reason; truth eternal tells me I've a mother there." *Hymnal* (Salt Lake City, UT: The Church of Jesus Christ of Latter-day Saints, 1985), 292.

I've a Mother Here   Inspired by Martin Pulido and Caroline Kline's 2014's Art and Poetry Contest, "A Mother Here," http://www.amotherhere.com/, as well as this lovely quote from President Harold B. Lee: "We forget that we have a Heavenly Father and a Heavenly Mother who are even more concerned, probably, than our earthly father and mother, and that influences from beyond are constantly working to try to help us when we do all we can." "The Influence and Responsibility of Women," *Relief Society Magazine* 51.2 (1964), 85.

In Which the Potter Imprints Herself   Isaiah 64:8 "But now, O Lord, thou art our father; we are the clay, and thou our potter; and we all are the work of thy hand."

Before   Jeremiah 1:5 "Before I formed thee in the belly I knew thee; and before thou camest forth out of the womb I sanctified thee, and I ordained thee a prophet unto the nations."

The Most Repeated Truths   In my research, the two most quoted passages on Heavenly Mother by General Authorities I found are: "All human beings—male and female—are created in the image of God. Each is a beloved spirit son or daughter of heavenly parents, and, as such, each has a divine nature and destiny." "The Family: A Proclamation to the World," The First Presidency and Council of the Twelve Apostles of The Church of Jesus Christ of Latter-day Saints (Salt Lake City, UT: The Church of Jesus Christ of Latter-day Saints, 1995).

And this one, by Orson F. Whitney: "No pain that we suffer, no trial that we experience is wasted. It ministers to our education, to the development of such qualities as patience, faith,

the house of Israel, how oft have I gathered you as a hen gathereth her chickens under her wings, and have nourished you."

She Came To Her   Matthew 26:37 "And he took with him Peter and the two sons of Zebedee, and began to be sorrowful and very heavy." Luke 22:43 "And there appeared an angel unto him from heaven, strengthening him."

Salt and Light   Matthew 5:13–15 "Ye are the salt of the earth: but if the salt have lost his savour, wherewith shall it be salted? it is thenceforth good for nothing, but to be cast out, and to be trodden under foot of men. Ye are the light of the world. A city that is set on an hill cannot be hid. Neither do men light a candle, and put it under a bushel, but on a candlestick; and it giveth light unto all that are in the house."

Her Repertoire   Inspired by Heather Sundahl, "Mourning Sickness: Dealing with Miscarriage," *The Exponent* blog, June 2, 2011, http://www.the-exponent.com/mourning-sickness-dealing-with-miscarriage/, and Liz Layton Johnson, "Reaching for Her," *By Common Consent* blog, May 5, 2012, https://bycommonconsent.com/2012/03/05/reaching-for-her/. Thanks to Carrie Stoddard Salisbury's help with the music terms.

Heavenly Doula   Inspired by Ryan Thomas, "My Search for the Divine Feminine," *The Exponent* 30.2 (2010), 25, http://www.exponentii.org/wp-content/uploads/2010/09/Fall-2010.pdf.

Mirror Image   Genesis 1:27 "So God created man in his own image, in the image of God created he him; male and female created he them."

Darkly   1 Corinthians 13:12 "For now we see through a glass, darkly; but then face to face: now I know in part; but then shall I know even as also I am known."

After Sleeping in the Forest   From Mary Oliver's poem, "Sleeping in the Forest." "I thought the earth remembered me, she took me back so tenderly, arranging her dark skirts, her pockets full of lichens and seeds. I slept as never before..." *New and Selected Poems* (Boston: Beacon Press, 1993).

What Jeffrey Taught Me   Jeffrey R. Holland, "[H]eavenly parents are reaching... across streams and mountains and deserts, anxious to hold us close." *However Long and Hard the Road* (Salt Lake City, UT: Deseret Book, 1985), 47.

The Mother Delights in Plainness   2 Nephi 31:3 "For my soul delighteth in plainness; for after this manner doth the Lord God work among the children of men. For the Lord God giveth light unto the understanding; for he speaketh unto men according to their language, unto their understanding."

What Jim Taught Me   Jim James, "His Master's Voice," *Monsters of Folk* (Shangri-La, 2009). "He sees his inner child. He hears his mother's voice softly calling. Spirit soldiers mother hovers. She holds up a paper cup. And the sound of life and love fills her ear."

A Planet and a Star   Antoine de Saint-Exupéry, *The Little Prince*, trans. by Richard Howard. "'What makes the desert beautiful,' the little prince said, 'is that it hides a well somewhere . . . '" I was surprised by suddenly understanding that mysterious radiance of the sands. When I was a little boy I lived in an old house, and there was a legend that a treasure was buried in it somewhere. Of course, no one was able to find the treasure, perhaps no one even searched. But it cast a spell over that whole house. My house hid a secret in the depths of its heart..." (New York: Houghton Mifflin Harcourt, 2000) 68.

My First Article of Faith   The First Article of Faith, "We believe in God, the Eternal Father, and in His Son, Jesus Christ, and in the Holy Ghost," *The Pearl of Great Price,* (Salt Lake City, UT: The Church of Jesus Christ of Latter-day Saints, 2013).

My Second   Young Women Theme, "I am a daughter of Heavenly Father, who loves me, and I love Him." (Salt Lake City, UT: The Church of Jesus Christ of Latter-day Saints, 1987).

Re-Turned   Malachi 4:5–6 "Behold, I will send you Elijah the prophet before the coming of the great and dreadful day of the Lord: And he shall turn the heart of the fathers to the children, and the heart of the children to their fathers . . . "

What J.P. Taught Me   Inspired by a friend, J.P. Haynie's / The Glendale Rabashaw's, beautiful song, "There's a Lighthouse."

As She Is   Moroni 7:48 "Wherefore, my beloved brethren, pray unto the Father with all the energy of heart, that ye may be filled with this love, which he hath bestowed upon all who are true followers of his Son, Jesus Christ; that ye may become the sons of God; that when he shall appear we shall be like him, for we shall see him as he is; that we may have this hope; that we may be purified even as he is pure. Amen."

Pink Moccasins   Inspired by Carol Lynn Pearson and her essay "A Walk in the Pink Moccasins," *Sunstone* 137 (2005), 21.

Mother-full   Inspired by: Carol Lynn Pearson, "A Motherless House," in *Women and Authority: Re-emerging Mormon Feminism,* ed. Maxine Hanks (Salt Lake City, UT: Signature Books, 1992), 232, Eliza R. Snow, "O My Father," Eliza R. Snow, *Hymnal* (Salt Lake City, UT: The Church of Jesus Christ of Latter-day Saints, 1985), 292, Joanna Brooks, "Invocation/Benediction," *Exponent II* 50.5 (2010), 18, Lisa Bolin Hawkin's "Another Prayer," *Exponent II* 6 (1980), 16, Margaret Rampton Munk's "First Grief," *Exponent II* 5.1 (1978), 17, and Melody Newey Johnson's "Heavenly Mother Sings," *"A Mother Here: Art and Poetry Contest," A Mother Here* (2013), http://www.amotherhere.com/coll/newey2.php#sthash.xLYmeBvz.dpbs.

Giants   Among them are Linda Wilcox, Margaret Toscano, Janice Allred, Maxine Hanks, Carol Lynn Pearson, Linda Sillitoe, Lisa Bolin Hawkins, Margaret Rampton Munk, Joanna Brooks, Nola Wallace, Margaret Barker, Martin Pulido, David Paulsen, Fiona Givens, and Melody Newey Johnson.

What Joanna Taught Me   Joanna Brooks, "God is a Mother and a Father. Mormon women matter." *The Book of Mormon Girl: A Memoir of an American* Faith (New York: Simon & Schuster, 2012), 140.

Eternal Life   John 17:3 "And this is life eternal, that they might know thee the only true God, and Jesus Christ, whom thou hast sent."

Mother Who Knows   Title from Julie B. Beck's, "Mothers Who Know," *Ensign,* October 2007; contents from 3 Nephi 13:33 "For your heavenly Father knoweth that ye have need of all these things."

What Moana Taught Me   Mark Mancina, "Know Who You Are," *Moana* (Walt Disney Records, 2016). "I have crossed the horizon to find you. I know your name. They have stolen the heart from inside you. But this does not define you. This is not who you are. You know who you are."

Photo credit: Jessica Peterson Photo

Rachel Hunt Steenblik researched Heavenly Mother full-time for the *BYU Studies* article, "'A Mother There': A Survey of Historical Teachings about Mother in Heaven." She also co-edited *Mormon Feminism: Essential Writings* for Oxford University Press and writes for *The Exponent* blog. She is a PhD student in philosophy of religion at Claremont Graduate University, and has a BA in philosophy from Brigham Young University and an MS in library and information science from Simmons College. She lives just outside of New York City with her husband and tiny children.

huntsteenblik.com   @rachelsteenblik

Ashley Mae Hoiland is the author and illustrator of *One Hundred Birds Taught Me to Fly*, the most recent publication in the Living Faith Series at the Maxwell Institute. Her artwork, children's books, public art projects and We Brave Women cards can be seen at ashmae .com. She received a BFA in studio art and an MFA in poetry, both from Brigham Young University. She is the mother of three small children and currently lives in Palo Alto, California.

🌐

ashmae.com

My Favorites

Made in the USA
San Bernardino, CA
29 July 2017